CARDIGANS & CLOSURES

Designs by
Melissa Leapman

Introduction

Would you like to perfect the art of the knitted jacket or cardigan? Join designer Melissa Leapman as she walks you through several closure techniques while you create seven beautiful jackets to wear and love. Master afterthought closures such as zippers and button loops, practice simple eyelet buttonholes and learn professional tips and tricks for double-thick button bands and amazing one-row buttonholes. You'll even discover the ins and outs of double-breasted closures and how to make your own handmade buttons to match your knitted fabric!

With the information here, you'll be knitting stunning garments with ideal closures each and every time.

Happy knitting!

Melissa

Melissa Leapman

Funky Boyfriend Cardigan, **page 37**

Table of Contents

Casual Jacket,
page 6

Rustic Jacket,
page 24

Rebecca,
page 32

Double-Breasted
Mosaic Cardi,
page 42

Part One:
KEEP IT SIMPLE WITH AFTERTHOUGHT CLOSURES

Sometimes it is a good idea to decide on closure details after the knitting is completed. After seaming, allow your garment to speak to you. Does it want a few oversized button loops? A sporty zipper? Traditional buttonholes? These techniques are explored in this section.

Button Loops

Button loops are suitable for projects when only a few buttons will be used, as seen in the Casual Jacket on page 6. Made close to the edge of the fabric, this type of closure can be custom sized to any button and is especially useful for extremely large buttons.

Overcast Button Loop

Step 1: Use pins to mark the placement for the beginning and end of each button loop. To make a foundation for a button loop, use a blunt-tip yarn needle to bring the yarn up from the wrong side to the right side at the lower marker, and then insert it down from the right side to the wrong side at the upper marker. Adjust the size of the loop by pulling on the yarn loop.

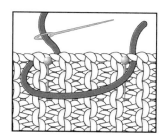

Step 2: To make the foundation sturdier, bring the needle up once more at the lower marker and back down again at the upper one. Repeat this step a third time if a stronger core is required, such as when using fine yarn.

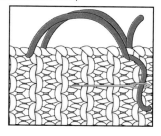

Step 3: Use buttonhole stitch (see page 31) to cover the foundation strands, working from the lower marker to the upper marker. Bring the yarn to the left of the needle, then insert the needle under all the loops and over the yarn, then pull the yarn up to tighten the stitch.

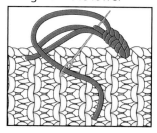

Zippers

It's simple to sew a zipper in by hand. This type of closure is used on the Tweedy Hoodie on page 11.

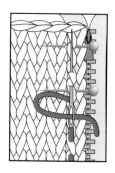

Step 1: With the zipper closed and the public side of the garment pieces facing you, pin the zipper into place. Then, use contrasting sewing thread to baste the zipper into place with a running stitch.

Step 2: Remove the pins and whipstitch the zipper tape to the wrong side of the garment.

Step 3: With the public side of the fabric facing you, backstitch the zipper to the knitted fabric.

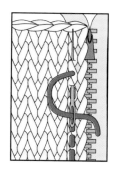

If there's any excess zipper tape at the top or bottom, fold it to the wrong side and tack it down. Remove basting thread. ●

Here's a textured car coat that uses overcast button loops as closures.
It is knitted out of bulky-weight yarn for quick and easy stitching.

Casual Jacket

Skill Level
■■□□ EASY

Sizes
Woman's small (medium, large, X-large,
2X-large, 3X-large)

Instructions are given for smallest size, with
larger sizes in parentheses. When only 1 number
is given, it applies to all sizes.

Finished Measurements
Chest (buttoned): 38 (42, 46, 50, 54, 58) inches
Length: 32 (32½, 33, 33½, 33½, 34) inches

Materials
- Lion Brand Alpine Wool (chunky weight; 77% wool/15% acrylic/ 8% rayon; 93 yds/3 oz per ball): 12 (14, 16, 18, 20, 22) balls oatmeal #223
- Size 9 (5.5mm) straight and 29-inch circular needles
- Size 10 (6mm) straight and 29-inch circular needles or size needed to obtain gauge
- Stitch holders
- 4 (2-inch) buttons #80712 from JHB International

Gauge
12 sts and 22 rows = 4 inches/10cm in Textured
pat with larger needles.

To save time, take time to check gauge.

Special Abbreviation
Make 1 (M1): Inc by making a backward loop over
RH needle.

Pattern Stitch
Textured (multiple of 3 sts + 2)
*Note: A chart is provided for the pat for those preferring
to work from charts.*
Row 1 (RS): P2, *k1, p2; rep from * end.
Row 2: K2, *p1, k2; rep from * to end.
Row 3: Knit.
Row 4: Purl.
Rep Rows 1–4 for pat.

Pattern Notes
All pieces are worked back and forth. Circular
needles may be used to accommodate stitches
of larger pieces; do not join.

Instructions include 1 selvage stitch at each
side; these stitches are not reflected in the
final measurements.

Work all shaping 1 stitch from the edge. Work
decreases as knit or purl decreases as necessary
to maintain the pattern.

Back
With larger circular needle, cast on 59 (65, 71, 77,
83, 89) sts.

Work even in Textured pat until piece measures
23½ inches, or desired length to underarm, ending
with a WS row.

Shape Armholes
Bind off 3 (4, 4, 5, 5, 6) sts at beg of next 2 rows,
then bind off 2 (2, 3, 3, 4, 4) sts at beg of following
2 rows—49 (53, 57, 61, 65, 69) sts.

Maintaining established pat, dec at each end on next
row, then [every RS row] 3 (4, 4, 5, 5, 6) times—41 (43,
47, 49, 53, 55) sts.

Work even until armholes measure 7 (7½, 8, 8½,
8½, 9) inches, ending with a WS row.

Shape Neck
Row 1 (RS): Work 11 (12, 14, 15, 17, 18) sts in pat; join 2nd ball of yarn and bind off 19 sts, work to end of row.

Row 2: Working both sides at once with separate balls of yarn, work even.

Maintaining established pat, dec 1 st at each neck edge once—10 (11, 13, 14, 16, 17) sts each side.

Work even until armholes measure 7½, (8, 8½, 9, 9, 9½) inches, ending with a WS row.

Shape Shoulders
Bind off 3 (4, 4, 5, 5, 6) sts at beg of next 4 rows, then bind off 4 (3, 5, 4, 6, 5) sts at beg of last 2 rows.

Pocket Lining
Make 2

With larger needles, cast on 15 (16, 15, 16, 15, 16) sts.

Work even in St st until piece measures 6 inches, ending with a WS row.

Slip sts onto holder.

Left Front
With larger needles, cast on 29 (32, 35, 38, 41, 44) sts.

Work even in Textured pat until piece measures 9 (9½, 10, 10½, 10½, 11) inches, ending with a WS row.

Place pocket lining (RS): Work 7 (8, 10, 11, 13, 14) sts, place next 15 (16, 15, 16, 15, 16) sts on st holder for pocket edging; maintaining established Textured pat, work across 15 (16, 15, 16, 15, 16) sts from pocket lining holder; work to end of row.

Work even until piece measures same as back to underarm, ending with a WS row.

Shape Armhole
At armhole edge, bind off 3 (4, 4, 5, 5, 6) sts once and 2 (2, 3, 3, 4, 4) sts once—24 (26, 28, 30, 32, 34) sts.

Maintaining established pat, dec 1 st at armhole edge [every RS row] 4 (5, 5, 6, 6, 7) times—20 (21, 23, 24, 26, 27) sts.

Work even until armhole measures 5½ (6, 6½, 7, 7, 7½) inches, ending with a RS row.

Shape Neck
At neck edge, bind off 3 sts once, and 2 sts twice—13 (14, 16, 17, 19, 20) sts.

At neck edge, dec 1 st [every RS row] 3 times—10 (11, 13, 14, 16, 17) sts.

Work even until armhole measures same as back to shoulders, ending with a WS row.

Shape Shoulder
At armhole edge, bind off 3 (4, 4, 5, 5, 6) sts twice, and 4 (3, 5, 4, 6, 5) sts once.

Right Front
Work same as left front to armholes, ending with a RS row.

Shape armholes same as for left front, then work even until armhole measures same as for left front to neck shaping, ending with a WS row.

Shape neck same as for left front, then work even until armhole measures same as for left front to shoulder shaping, ending with a RS row.

Shape shoulders same as for left front.

Sleeves
With larger needles, cast on 32 sts.

Work in Textured pat; working new sts into pat as they accumulate, inc 1 st each side [every 8 rows] 0 (0, 0, 0, 7, 12) times, [every 10 rows] 0 (0, 0, 6, 4, 0) times, [every 12 rows] 0 (0, 8, 3, 0, 0) times, [every 16 rows] 0 (6, 0, 0, 0, 0) times, [every 18 rows] 2 (0, 0, 0, 0, 0) times, then [every 20 rows] 3 (0, 0, 0, 0, 0) times as follows: K1, M1, work in pat to last st, M1, k1—42 (44, 48, 50, 54, 56) sts.

Work even until sleeve measures 18½ inches or desired length to underarm, ending with a WS row.

Shape Cap
Bind off 3 (4, 4, 5, 5, 6) sts at beg of next 2 rows—36 (36, 40, 40, 44, 44) sts.

Maintaining established pat, dec 1 st at armhole edge [every 4 rows] 2 (3, 2, 4, 2, 3) times, then [every RS row] 8 (7, 10, 8, 12, 11) times—16 sts.

Work 0 (0, 1, 0, 0, 0) row(s) even.

Bind off 2 sts at beg of next 4 rows—8 sts.

Bind off.

Finishing
Weave in ends. Block pieces to measurements.

Sew shoulder seams.

Neckband

With RS facing and smaller circular needle, pick up and knit 56 sts along neckline.

Row 1 (WS): Knit.

Row 2: Purl.

Bind off kwise on WS.

Sleeve Edging

With RS facing and smaller needles, pick up and knit 28 sts along cast-on edge of sleeve.

Work as for neckband.

Set in sleeves.

Sew sleeve seams.

Sew side seams.

Lower Edging

With RS facing and smaller circular needle, pick up and knit 114 (126, 138, 150, 162, 174) sts along bottom edge.

Work as for neckband.

Left Front Edging

With RS facing and smaller circular needle, pick up and knit 110 (112, 114, 116, 116, 118) sts along left front edge.

Work as for neckband.

Right Front Edging

With RS facing and smaller circular needle, pick up and knit 110 (112, 114, 116, 116, 118) sts along right front edge.

Work as for neckband.

Pocket Edgings

With RS facing and smaller needles, knit 15 (16, 15, 16, 15, 16) sts from pocket holder.

Work as for neckband.

Sew sides of pocket edging to RS of front.

Rep for other pocket edging.

Sew pocket linings to WS of fronts.

Button Loops

Mark positions for 4 button loops on right front, with the first 1½ inches from beg of front neck shaping, the last 17 inches from beg of front neck shaping, and the others evenly spaced between the 2.

Make overcast button loops (see page 5) on right front at marked positions. Sew on buttons. ●

STITCH KEY
☐ K on RS, p on WS
⊟ P on RS, k on WS

3-st rep

TEXTURED PATTERN CHART

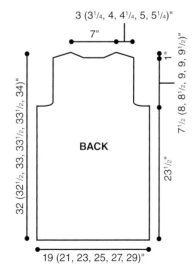

3 (3¼, 4, 4¼, 5, 5¼)"

7"

1"

7½ (8, 8½, 9, 9, 9½)"

32 (32½, 33, 33½, 33½, 34)"

23½"

BACK

19 (21, 23, 25, 27, 29)"

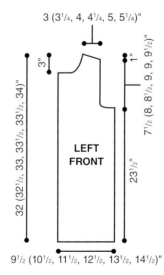

3 (3¼, 4, 4¼, 5, 5¼)"

3"

1"

7½ (8, 8½, 9, 9, 9½)"

32 (32½, 33, 33½, 33½, 34)"

23½"

LEFT FRONT

9½ (10½, 11½, 12½, 13½, 14½)"

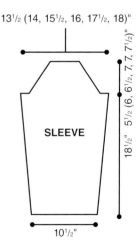

13½ (14, 15½, 16, 17½, 18)"

18½ 5½ (6, 6½, 7, 7, 7½)"

SLEEVE

10½"

LESSON TWO: INSERTING A ZIPPER

Adding a zipper to your finished garment is a cinch once you get the hang of the process. Turn to page 5 for a quick tutorial.

Tweedy Hoodie

Skill Level
■■□□ EASY

Sizes
Woman's small (medium, large, X-large, 2X-large, 3X-large)

Instructions are given for smallest size, with larger sizes in parentheses. When only 1 number is given, it applies to all sizes.

Finished Measurements
Chest (zipped): 35 (39, 42, 46, 49, 53) inches
Length: 27 inches

Materials
- Cascade Yarn Cascade 220 (worsted weight; 100% wool; 220 yds/100g per skein): 5 (6, 6, 7, 8, 9) skeins marine blue #8339 (A) and 3 (3, 4, 4, 5, 5) skeins each summer sky #7815 (B) and natural #8010 (C)
- Size 9 (5.5mm) straight, 24- and 36-inch circular needles or size needed to obtain gauge
- Stitch holders
- Stitch markers
- 24-inch zipper

4 MEDIUM

Gauge
18 sts and 32 rows = 4 inches/10cm in Slip St pat.

To save time, take time to check gauge.

Special Abbreviation
Make 1 (M1): Inc by making a backward loop over RH needle.

Pattern Stitch

Slip St (multiple of 4 sts + 3)
Row 1 (RS): With B, k3, *sl 1 wyib, k3; rep from * to end.
Row 2: With B, k3, *sl 1 wyif, k3; rep from * to end.
Row 3: With A, k1, sl 1 wyib, *k3, sl 1 wyib; rep from * to last st, k1.
Row 4: With A, k1, sl 1 wyif, *k3, sl 1 wyif; rep from * to last st, k1.
Rows 5 and 6: With C, rep Rows 1 and 2.
Rows 7 and 8: With A, rep Rows 3 and 4.
Rep Rows 1–8 for pat.

Special Technique

3-Needle Bind-Off: With RS tog and needles parallel, using a 3rd needle, knit tog a st from the front needle with 1 from the back. *Knit tog a st from the front and back needles, and slip the first st over the 2nd to bind off; rep from * across, then fasten off last st.

Pattern Note

All pieces are worked back and forth. Circular needles may be used to accommodate the number of stitches of larger pieces; do not join.

Back

With A, cast on 79 (87, 95, 103, 111, 119) sts.

Purl 1 WS row.

Change to B; work even in Slip St pat until back measures 18 (17½, 17, 17, 16½, 16½) inches or desired length to underarm, ending with a WS row.

Shape Armholes

Bind off 4 (5, 6, 7, 7, 8) sts at beg of next 2 rows, then bind off 2 (2, 3, 3, 4, 4) sts at beg of following 2 rows—67 (73, 77, 83, 89, 95) sts.

Dec row (RS): Ssk, work in established pat to last 2 sts, k2tog—65 (71, 75, 81, 87, 93) sts.

Rep Dec row [every RS row] 1 (0, 0, 1, 3, 5) time(s), then [every 4th row] 2 (3, 3, 3, 2, 1) time(s)—59 (65, 69, 73, 77, 81) sts.

Work even until armhole measures 8 (8½, 9, 9, 9½, 9½) inches, ending with a WS row.

Shape Shoulders

Bind off 4 (4, 5, 5, 6, 6) sts at beg of next 6 rows and 2 (5, 4, 6, 5, 7) sts at beg of following 2 rows—31 sts.

Bind off.

Pocket Linings
Make 2

With A, cast on 25 sts.

Work even in St st until piece measures 4½ inches, ending with a WS row.

Slip sts onto holder.

Left Front

With A, cast on 39 (43, 47, 51, 55, 59) sts.

Purl 1 row.

Change to B; work even in Slip St pat until piece measures 5 inches, ending with a WS row.

Place pocket lining (RS): Work across 7 (9, 11, 13, 15, 17) sts; place next 25 sts on st holder for pocket edging; work in established Slip St pat across 25 pocket lining sts; work to end of row.

Work even until piece measures same as back to underarm, ending with a WS row.

Shape Armhole

At armhole edge, bind off 4 (5, 6, 7, 7, 8) sts once and 2 (2, 3, 3, 4, 4) sts once—33 (36, 38, 41, 44, 47) sts.

Work 1 row even.

Dec row (RS): Ssk, work to end of row—32 (35, 37, 40, 43, 46) sts.

Rep Dec row [every RS row] 1 (0, 0, 1, 3, 5) time(s), then [every 4 rows] 2 (3, 3, 3, 2, 1) time(s)—29 (32, 34, 36, 38, 40) sts.

Work even until armhole measures 6 (6½, 7, 7, 7½, 7½) inches, ending with a RS row.

Shape Neck

Row 1 (WS): Work 7 sts and slip them onto a holder; work to end of row—22 (25, 27, 29, 31, 33) sts.

Note: Note last pattern row worked on front neck sts.

At neck edge, bind off 3 sts once and 2 sts once, then dec 1 st [every row] 3 times—14 (17, 19, 21, 23, 25) sts.

Work even until armhole measures same as back to shoulders, ending with a WS row.

Shape Neck

Row 1 (RS): Slip first 7 sts onto a holder; rejoin yarn and work to end of row—22 (25, 27, 29, 31, 33) sts.

At neck edge, bind off 3 sts once and 2 sts once, then dec 1 st [every row] 3 times—14 (17, 19, 21, 23, 25) sts.

Work even until armhole measures same as back to shoulders, ending with a RS row.

Shape Shoulders

At armhole edge, bind off 4 (4, 5, 5, 6, 6) sts 3 times and 2 (5, 4, 6, 5, 7) sts once.

Sleeves

With A, cast on 79 (79, 83, 83, 87, 87) sts.

Purl 1 row.

Change to B; work 14 rows even in Slip St pat.

Dec row (RS): Ssk, work to last 2 sts, k2tog—77 (77, 81, 81, 85, 85) sts.

Rep Dec row [every 14 (18, 18, 18, 18, 18) rows] 9 (7, 7, 7, 7, 7) times—59 (63, 67, 67, 71, 71) sts.

Work even until piece measures 18½ inches or desired length to underarm, ending with a WS row.

Shape Cap

Bind off 4 (5, 6, 7, 7, 8) sts at beg of next 2 rows—51 (53, 55, 53, 57, 55) sts.

Dec row (RS): Ssk, work to last 2 sts, k2tog—49 (51, 53, 51, 55, 53) sts.

Rep Dec row [every 4 rows] 6 (7, 8, 9, 9, 10) times, then [every other row] 6 (6, 6, 4, 6, 4) times—25 sts.

Work 1 row even.

Bind off 3 sts at beg of next 4 rows—13 sts.

Bind off.

Finishing

Weave in all ends.

Block all pieces to finished measurements.

Pocket Edgings

Row 1 (RS): With RS facing and A, knit across 25 sts from pocket edging holder.

Row 2 (WS): Knit across.

Row 3: Purl across.

Bind off kwise on WS.

Rep for 2nd pocket edging.

Shape Shoulders

At armhole edge, bind off 4 (4, 5, 5, 6, 6) sts 3 times and 2 (5, 4, 6, 5, 7) sts once.

Right Front

With A, cast on 39 (43, 47, 51, 55, 59) sts.

Work same as for left front to underarm, ending with a RS row.

Shape Armhole

At armhole edge, bind off 4 (5, 6, 7, 7, 8) sts once and 2 (2, 3, 3, 4, 4) sts once—33 (36, 38, 41, 44, 47) sts.

Dec row (RS): Work to last 2 sts, k2tog—32 (35, 37, 40, 43, 46) sts.

Rep Dec row [every RS row] 1 (0, 0, 1, 3, 5) time(s), then [every 4 rows] 2 (3, 3, 3, 2, 1) time(s)—29 (32, 34, 36, 38, 40) sts.

Work even until armhole measures 6 (6½, 7, 7, 7½, 7½) inches, ending with same WS pat row as noted for left front neck sts. Cut yarn.

Sew sides of pocket edgings to front.

Sew pocket linings to WS of front.

Sew shoulder seams.

Hood

With RS facing and A, knit across 7 sts from the right front neck holder; pick up and knit 17 sts along right front neck, 31 sts along back of neck and 17 sts along left front neck; knit across 7 sts from left front neck holder—79 sts.

Knit 1 row.

Begin Slip St pat with the row after the pat row noted at the front neck shaping; work even for 8 rows, and on last row, work 39 sts, pm, k1, pm, work to end of row.

Shape Back Hood

Note: Work all sts before first marker and after 2nd marker in established Slip St pat; work all sts between markers in garter st.

Row 1 (inc, RS): Work to first marker, slip marker, M1, k1, M1, slip marker, work to end of row—81 sts.

Rows 2–12: Slipping markers, work to first marker, k3, work to end of row.

Row 13 (inc): Work to first marker; [k1, M1] twice, k1; work to end of row—83 sts.

Rows 14–24: Slipping markers, work to first marker, k5, work to end of row.

Row 25 (inc): Work to first marker; k2, M1, k1, M1, k2; work to end of row—85 sts.

Row 26: Slipping markers, work to first marker, k7, work to end of row.

Work even until hood measures 12 inches, ending with a WS row.

Dec back hood as follows:

Row 1 (dec, RS): Work to first marker; k1, ssk, k1, k2tog, k1; work to end of row—83 sts.

Rows 2, 4 and 6: Work even, knitting sts between markers.

Row 3 (dec): Work to first marker; ssk, k1, k2tog; work to end of row—81 sts.

Row 5 (dec): Work to first marker; sk2p; work to end of row—79 sts.

Row 7 (dec): Removing both markers when you come to them, work to first marker, ssk, work to end of row—78 sts.

Divide rem sts onto 2 dpns with 39 sts on each; with WS facing, work 3-needle bind-off.

Front Edging

With RS facing, circular needle and A, and beg at the lower right front edge, pick up and knit 107 sts along right front edge, 114 sts along front of hood, and 107 sts along left front edge—328 sts.

Row 1 (WS): Sl 1, knit to end.

Row 2 (RS): Sl 1, purl to end.

Bind-off row: Sl 1, then knit and bind off across.

Set in sleeves.

Sew underarm and side seams, leaving lower 5 inches of side seams open for side slits.

Weave in rem ends.

Sew in zipper (see page 5). ●

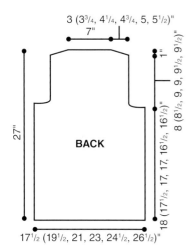

3 (3³/₄, 4¹/₄, 4³/₄, 5, 5¹/₂)"

7"

1"

8 (8¹/₂, 9, 9, 9¹/₂, 9¹/₂)"

27"

18 (17¹/₂, 17, 17, 16¹/₂, 16¹/₂)"

BACK

17¹/₂ (19¹/₂, 21, 23, 24¹/₂, 26¹/₂)"

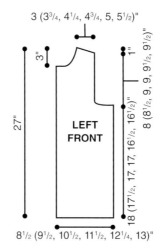

3 (3³/₄, 4¹/₄, 4³/₄, 5, 5¹/₂)"

3"

1"

8 (8¹/₂, 9, 9, 9¹/₂, 9¹/₂)"

27"

18 (17¹/₂, 17, 17, 16¹/₂, 16¹/₂)"

LEFT FRONT

8¹/₂ (9¹/₂, 10¹/₄, 11¹/₂, 12¹/₄, 13)"

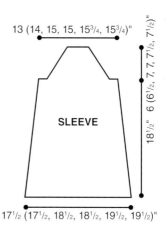

13 (14, 15, 15, 15³/₄, 15³/₄)"

6 (6¹/₂, 7, 7, 7¹/₂, 7¹/₂)"

18¹/₂"

SLEEVE

17¹/₂ (17¹/₂, 18¹/₂, 18¹/₂, 19¹/₂, 19¹/₂)"

Part Two:
BUTTONHOLE ESSENTIALS

Knitters have several buttonhole methods to choose from.
Eyelets and standard bound-off buttonholes are the first ones to master.

Eyelet Buttonholes
Simple yarn overs create the easiest kind of buttonholes. The size of eyelet buttonholes depends on the size of the yarn and needles used. They're often used on babies' and kids' garments, but can add a soft, romantic effect to womens wear as seen in Le Charme on page 19.

Simple One-Stitch Eyelet Buttonhole
Mark positions for buttonholes along front edge.

Buttonhole row (RS):
*Work to marked buttonhole position, k2tog, yo; repeat from * to create the number of desired buttonholes, work to end of row.

Two-Stitch Eyelet Buttonhole
Mark positions for buttonholes along front edge.

Buttonhole row (RS):
*Work to marked buttonhole position, k2tog, [yo] twice, ssk; repeat from * to create the number of desired button-holes, work to end of row.

Vertical Eyelet Buttonhole
Buttonhole row 1 (RS): *Work to marked buttonhole position, k2tog, yo; repeat from * to create the number of desired buttonholes, work to end of row.

Buttonhole row 2: *Work to buttonhole, knit (or purl, depending on the stitch pattern), then yo; repeat from * for all buttonholes, work to end of row.

Buttonhole row 3: *Work to buttonhole, knit (or purl, depending on the stitch pattern) directly into the eyelet hole itself, drop the stitch that's above the eyelet on the left-hand needle; repeat from * for all buttonholes, work to end of row.

CLOSURES UP CLOSE
In most cases, pattern instructions tell you to space buttons and buttonholes evenly along the front edges of a garment. Here's how:

Step 1: Place markers for the top and bottom buttons.

Step 2: Use a tape measure to determine the length between these two markers.

Step 3: Determine how many spaces will be required between the remaining buttons. There will be one more space than there will be buttons. For example, if you are planning seven buttons total, there will be five buttons between the top and bottom ones, with six spaces in between them.

Step 4: Divide the length between the top and bottom markers by the number of spaces needed. Voilà! That is how far apart the remaining buttons will be from each other. Place markers for the remaining buttons.

Elongated Vertical Eyelet Buttonhole
(used in Le Charme on page 19 on a ribbed band)

Buttonhole row 1 (RS): *Work to marked buttonhole position, [yo] twice, k2tog; repeat from * to create the number of desired buttonholes, work to end of row.

Buttonhole row 2: *Work to buttonhole, knit (or purl, depending on the stitch pattern) into the first yo, drop the second yo; repeat from * for all buttonholes, work to end of row.

Buttonhole row 3: Work to buttonhole, knit (or purl, depending on the stitch pattern) directly into the eyelet hole itself, drop the stitch that's above the eyelet on the left-hand needle; repeat from * for all buttonholes, work to end of row.

Simple Bound-Off Buttonholes

This type of buttonhole is worked over two rows. First, a number of stitches are bound off, and then, on the subsequent row the same number of stitches is cast on. Easy!

Step 1: On the first row, work in the pattern to where the buttonhole is to be. Then, bind off the required number of stitches.

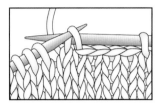

Step 2: On the next row, work in pattern to the buttonhole, then cast on the same number of stitches as were bound off on the previous row. ●

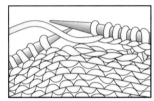

Finished Simple Bound-Off Buttonhole

Overcast Stitch

To reinforce a simple eyelet buttonhole, especially if the yarn is particularly stretchy, use the following technique:

Using a blunt-tip yarn needle and matching yarn or thread, make short whipstitches close together all around the opening of the eyelet hole.

CLOSURES UP CLOSE

Although eyelet buttonholes can be used in any stitch pattern, they are great when worked in 1x1 rib. If you make the yarn over in a recessed purl "valley," the hole will remain invisible until it is actually used as a buttonhole. Bonus!

On the Pick Up

In many cases, the front bands of cardigans and jackets are added after the garment pieces have been knitted. This means that stitches must be picked up along the edge of the fabric. Here's how:

Step 1: With the right side of the fabric facing you, insert a knitting needle into the first row of the fabric, working between the selvage stitch and the second stitch. Wrap the yarn around the needle knitwise.

Step 2: Draw the yarn through the main fabric to create one knit stitch on the needle.

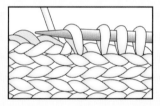

Repeat Steps 1 and 2 to pick up stitches along the edge of the fabric, allowing the selvage stitches to roll to the wrong side.

Depending on the relationship between the stitch and row gauges, you will want to occasionally skip a row on the main fabric to prevent the picked-up band from becoming too long. For example, if your row gauge is 6 rows per inch and the stitch gauge of your band is 4 stitches per inch, pick up 2 stitches for every 3 rows along the front edge of your cardigan.

LESSON ONE: EYELET BUTTONHOLES

Sometimes a simple eyelet buttonhole is the perfect closure to a cardigan. Practice this essential (but relatively simple) buttonhole technique as you knit this useful wardrobe piece.

Le Charme

Skill Level

 INTERMEDIATE

Sizes

Woman's small (medium, large, X-large, 2X-large, 3X-large)

Instructions are given for smallest size, with larger sizes in parentheses. When only 1 number is given, it applies to all sizes.

Finished Measurements
Sweater
Bust (buttoned): 36½ (38½, 42½, 44½, 46½, 52½) inches
Length: 23 (23, 23½, 23½, 23½, 24) inches

Scarf: 4½ x 67½ inches

Materials

- Classic Elite Woodland (DK weight; 65% wool/35% nettles; 131 yds/ 50g per skein): 13 (13, 14, 15, 16, 17) balls violet #3195
- Size 5 (3.75mm) straight and 32-inch circular needles
- Size 6 (4mm) straight needles or size needed to obtain gauge
- 9 custom buttons from Bejeweled & Bedazzled

Gauge

24 sts and 29 rows = 4 inches/10cm in Lace pat with larger needles.

To save time, take time to check gauge.

Special Abbreviations

Centered double dec (CDD): Sl 2 as if to k2tog, k1, pass the 2 slipped sts over.

Slip, slip, purl (ssp): Slip next 2 sts 1 at a time kwise, slip sts back to LH needle and p2tog-tbl.

Make 1 Left (M1L): Insert LH needle from front to back under the running thread between the last st worked and next st on LH needle; knit into the back of resulting loop.

Make 1 Right (M1R): Insert LH needle from back to front under the running thread between the last st worked and next st on LH needle. With RH needle, knit into the front of resulting loop.

Pattern Stitches

1x1 Rib (odd number of sts)
Row 1 (RS): K1, *p1, k1; rep from * to end.
Row 2: P1, *k1, p1; rep from * to end.
Rep Rows 1 and 2 for pat.

Lace (multiple of 12 sts + 5)
Note: A chart is provided for those preferring to work pat st from a chart.
Row 1 (RS): K1, yo, CDD, yo, *k3, p3, k3, yo, CDD, yo; rep from * to last st, k1.
Rows 2 and 4: P1, *p6, k3, p3; rep from * to last 4 sts, p4.
Row 3: *K4, *yo, ssk, k1, p3, k1, k2tog, yo, k3; rep from * to last st, k1.
Rows 5–8: Rep Rows 1–4.
Row 9: Rep Row 1.
Row 10: P1, *k3, p3; rep from * to last 4 sts, k3, p1.
Row 11: K1, p3, *k3, yo, CDD, yo, k3, p3; rep from * to last st, k1.
Rows 12 and 14: P1, *k3, p9; rep from * to last 4 sts, k3, p1.
Row 13: K1, p3, *k1, k2tog, yo, k3, yo, ssk, k1, p3; rep from * to last st, k1.
Rows 15–18: Rep Rows 11–14.
Row 19: Rep Row 11.
Row 20: Rep Row 10.
Rep Rows 1–20 for pat.

Pattern Notes

All pieces are worked back and forth. Circular needles may be used to accommodate stitches of larger pieces; do not join.

The Lace pattern is formed by paired decreases and yarn overs. When shaping in Lace pattern, if you cannot work both the decrease and the yarn over(s), work in stockinette stitch.

Work all shaping decreases as follows: On right-side rows, k1, ssk, work to last 3 stitches, k2tog, k1; on wrong-side rows, p1, p2tog, work to last 3 stitches, ssp, p1.

Back

With smaller needles, cast on 101 (113, 113, 125, 137, 149) sts.

Work in 1x1 Rib until piece measures ¾ inch, ending with a WS row.

Change to larger needles and Lace pat; work even until piece measures 13½ inches or desired length to underarm, ending with a WS row.

Shape Armholes

Bind off 12 (12, 12, 18, 18, 24) sts at beg of next 2 rows—77 (89, 89, 89, 101, 101) sts.

Work even until armholes measure 8½ (8½, 9, 9, 9, 9½) inches, ending with a WS row.

Shape Shoulders

Bind off 5 (6, 6, 6, 7, 7) sts at beg of next 6 rows and 3 (6, 6, 6, 9, 9) sts at beg of following 2 rows—41 sts.

Bind off.

Left Front

With smaller needles, cast on 53 (53, 65, 65, 65, 66) sts.

Work in 1x1 Rib until piece measures ¾ inch, ending with a WS row.

Change to larger needles and Lace pat; work even until piece measures same as back to underarm, ending with a WS row.

Shape Armhole

Bind off 12 (12, 12, 18, 18, 24) sts at beg of next row—41 (41, 53, 47, 47, 53) sts.

Work even until armhole measures 6½ (6½, 7, 7, 7, 7½) inches, ending with a RS row.

Shape Neck

At neck edge, bind off 11 (9, 13, 11, 9, 11) sts once, and 7 (4, 10, 7, 4, 7) sts once—23 (28, 30, 29, 34, 35) sts.

At neck edge, dec 1 st [every row] 3 (1, 5, 3, 1, 3) time(s), then [every other row] 2 (3, 1, 2, 3, 2) time(s)—18 (24, 24, 24, 30, 30) sts.

Work even until armhole measures 8½ (8½, 9, 9, 9, 9½) inches, ending with a WS row.

Shape Shoulder

At armhole edge, bind off 5 (6, 6, 6, 7, 7) sts 3 times and 3 (6, 6, 6, 9, 9) sts once.

Right Front

Work same as for left front to underarm, ending with a RS row.

Work armhole same as for left front to neck shaping, ending with a WS row.

Shape neck as for left front, ending with a RS row.

Shape shoulder as for left front.

Sleeves

With smaller needles, cast on 53 sts.

Work 4 rows in 1x1 Rib.

Change to larger needles and Lace pat; working new sts into Lace pat as they accumulate, inc 1 st each side [every RS row] 0 (0, 0, 0, 0, 4) times, [every 4 rows] 4 (2, 14, 17, 23, 27) times, then [every 6 rows] 20 (22, 14, 11, 5, 0) times as follows: k1, M1R, work to last st, M1L, k1—101 (101, 109, 109, 109, 115) sts.

Work even until piece measures 22 (22½, 22½, 22½, 21, 21) inches, ending with a WS row.

Bind off in pat.

Scarf

With smaller needles, cast on 29 sts.

Work 4 rows in 1x1 Rib.

Change to larger needles and Lace pat; work even until piece measures 67½ inches, ending with Row 10 or Row 20 of pat.

Change to smaller needles; work 4 rows in 1x1 Rib.

Bind off in rib.

Finishing

Weave in ends. Block all pieces to finished measurements.

Sew shoulder seams.

Neckband

With RS facing and smaller circular needle, pick up and knit 125 sts along neckline.

Work 1x1 Rib for 1 inch.

Bind off in rib.

Button Band

With RS facing and smaller circular needle, pick up and knit 119 (119, 121, 121, 121, 123) sts along left front.

Work 1x1 Rib for 1½ inches.

Bind off in rib.

Buttonhole Band

Mark positions for 9 evenly spaced buttonholes along right front edge, with first and last markers being ½ inch from top and bottom.

With RS facing and smaller circular needle, pick up and knit 119 (119, 121, 121, 121, 123) sts along right front.

Rows 1–6: Work in 1x1 Rib.

Row 7 (Buttonhole row RS): *Work to marked buttonhole position (ending after a knit st), yo twice; k2tog; rep from * 8 times, work to end.

Row 8: *Work to next double yo (ending after a purl st), knit first yo, drop 2nd yo; rep from * 8 times, work to end.

Row 9: *Work to buttonhole, yo, purl into yo and drop next st from LH needle; rep from * 8 times, work to end.

Work even until band measures 1½ inches.

Bind off in rib.

Loop for Scarf

With smaller needles, cast on 4 sts.

Row 1 (RS): P1, k2, p1.

Row 2: K1, p2, k1.

Rep Row 1 and 2 until piece measures 1½ inches.

Bind off.

Sew loop onto the back of sweater, with one edge at the top of neck rib and other edge at rib pick-up row.

Set in sleeves.

Sew underarm and side seams.

Sew on buttons opposite buttonholes.

Work overcast st (see page 18) around buttonholes.

Pull scarf through loop, positioning as desired. •

STITCH KEY

☐	K on RS, p on WS
−	P on RS, k on WS
O	Yo
⋏	CDD
╲	Ssk
╱	K2tog

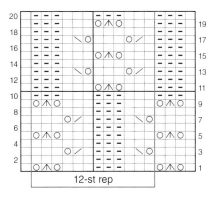

LACE CHART

12-st rep

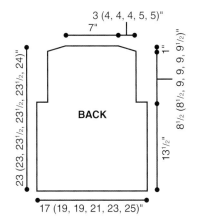

BACK

3 (4, 4, 4, 5, 5)"
7"
1"
8½ (8½, 9, 9, 9, 9½)"
23 (23, 23½, 23½, 23½, 24)"
13½"
17 (19, 19, 21, 23, 25)"

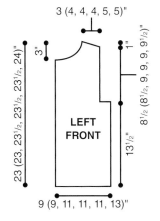

LEFT FRONT

3 (4, 4, 4, 5, 5)"
3"
1"
8½ (8½, 9, 9, 9, 9½)"
23 (23, 23½, 23½, 23½, 24)"
13½"
9 (9, 11, 11, 11, 13)"

SLEEVE

17 (17, 18, 18, 18, 19)"
22 (22½, 22½, 22½, 21, 21)"
9"

Every knitter needs a good, basic buttonhole in their repertoire. The three-row version that's used in this stockinette jacket is quite versatile and easy to do.

Rustic Jacket

Skill Level
■ ■ □ □ EASY

Sizes
Woman's small (medium, large, X-large, 2X-large, 3X-large)

Instructions are given for smallest size, with larger sizes in parentheses. When only 1 number is given, it applies to all sizes.

Finished Measurements
Chest (buttoned): 36 (40, 44, 48, 52, 56) inches
Length: 22 (22½, 23, 23½, 23½, 24) inches

Materials
- Berroco Peruvia (Aran weight; 100% Peruvian highland wool; 174 yds/100g per hank): 6 (7, 7, 8, 8, 9) hanks prairie dog #7105 (A) and 1 (1, 1, 1, 2, 2) hank(s) saddle brown #7152 (B)
- Size 9 (5.5mm) needles
- Size 10 (6mm) needles or size needed to obtain gauge
- 7 (25mm) buttons #310213 from Dill Buttons of America
- 7 small round buttons (optional)

Gauge
18 sts and 22 rows = 4 inches/10cm in St st with larger needles.

To save time, take time to check gauge.

Special Abbreviations
Slip, slip, purl (ssp): Slip next 2 sts 1 at a time kwise, slip sts back to LH needle and p2tog-tbl.

Make 1 Left (M1L): Insert LH needle from front to back under the running thread between the last st worked and next st on LH needle; knit into the back of resulting loop.

Make 1 Right (M1R): Insert LH needle from back to front under the running thread between the last st worked and next st on LH needle. With RH needle, knit into the front of resulting loop.

Pattern Notes
Instructions include 1 selvage stitch each side; these stitches are not included on the schematics or in the final measurements.

Work all decreases as follows: On right-side rows, k2, ssk, knit to last 4 stitches, k2tog, k2; on wrong-side rows, p2, p2tog, purl to last 4 stitches, ssp, p2.

All pieces are worked back and forth. Circular needles may used to accommodate stitches of larger pieces; do not join.

Back
With smaller needles and B, cast on 70 (78, 85, 93, 100, 109) sts.

Working in garter st (knit all rows), work [2 rows B, 2 rows A] twice, 2 rows B and on last row, inc 12 (14, 15, 17, 18, 19) sts evenly across—82 (92, 100, 110, 118, 128) sts.

Change to larger needles and A; work even in St st until piece measures 13½ inches or desired length to underarm, ending with a WS row.

Shape Armholes
Bind off 4 (5, 6, 7, 8, 9) sts at beg of next 2 rows, then bind off 2 (3, 3, 4, 5, 6) sts at beg of following 2 rows—70 (76, 82, 88, 92, 98) sts.

Dec 1 st each side (see Pattern Notes) [every row] twice, then [every other row] 4 (5, 6, 7, 7, 8) times—58 (62, 66, 70, 74, 78) sts.

Work even until armholes measure 7½ (8, 8½, 9, 9, 9½) inches, ending with a WS row.

Shape Shoulders

Bind off 4 (5, 6, 6, 7, 8) sts at beg of next 4 rows—42 (42, 42, 46, 46, 46) sts.

Bind off 5 (5, 5, 6, 6, 6) sts at beg of next 2 rows—32 (32, 32, 34, 34, 34) sts.

Bind off.

Left Front

With smaller needles and B, cast on 34 (37, 41, 44, 49, 53) sts.

Working in garter st (knit all rows), work [2 rows B, 2 rows A] twice, 2 rows B and on last row, inc 6 (7, 7, 8, 9, 9) sts evenly across—40 (44, 48, 52, 58, 62) sts.

Change to larger needles and A; work even in St st until piece measures same as back to underarm, ending with a WS row.

Shape Armhole

At armhole edge, bind off 4 (5, 6, 7, 8, 9) sts once, then 2 (3, 3, 4, 5, 6) sts once—34 (36, 39, 41, 45, 47) sts.

Dec 1 st at armhole edge [every row] twice, then [every other row] 4 (5, 6, 7, 7, 8) times—28 (29, 31, 32, 36, 37) sts.

Work even until armhole measures 5½ (6, 6½, 7, 7, 7½) inches, ending with a RS row.

Shape Neck

At neck edge, bind off 6 (5, 5, 4, 6, 5) sts once, 4 sts once and 3 sts once—15 (17, 19, 21, 23, 25) sts.

Dec 1 st at neck edge [every row] twice—13 (15, 17, 19, 21, 23) sts.

Work even until armhole measures 7½ (8, 8½, 9, 9, 9½) inches, ending with a WS row.

Shape Shoulders

At armhole edge, bind off 4 (5, 6, 6, 7, 8) sts twice and 5 (5, 5, 7, 7, 7) sts once.

Right Front

Work same as for left front to underarm, ending with a RS row.

Shape armholes as for right front, then work even until armhole measures 5½ (6, 6½, 7, 7, 7½) inches, ending with a WS row.

Shape neck as for left front, then work even until armhole measures 7½ (8, 8½, 9, 9, 9½) inches, ending with a RS row.

Shape shoulders as for left front.

Sleeves

With smaller needles and B, cast on 37 sts.

Working in garter st (knit all rows), work [2 rows B, 2 rows A] twice, 2 rows B and on last row, inc 7 sts evenly across—44 sts.

Change to larger needles and St st; work 10 (8, 6, 4, 4, 4) rows even.

Inc row (RS): K1, M1R, knit to last st, M1L, k1—46 sts.

Rep Inc row [every 4 rows] 0 (0, 0, 0, 6, 12) times, [every 6 rows] 0 (0, 3, 14, 10, 6) times, [every 8 rows] 0 (5, 8, 0, 0, 0) times, [every 10 rows] 3 (4, 0, 0, 0, 0) times, and [every 12 rows] 4 (0, 0, 0, 0, 0) times—60 (64, 68, 74, 78, 82) sts.

Work even until sleeve measures 18½ inches or desired length to underarm, ending with a WS row.

Shape Cap

Bind off 4 (5, 6, 7, 8, 9) sts at beg of next 2 rows—52 (54, 56, 60, 62, 64) sts.

Dec 1 st each side [every other row] 10 (11, 13, 14, 13, 15) times, then [every row] 4 (4, 3, 4, 6, 5) times—24 sts.

Bind off 2 sts at beg of next 6 rows—12 sts.

Bind off.

Finishing
Weave in ends.

Block all pieces.

Sew shoulder seams.

Neckband
With RS facing, smaller needles and B, pick up and knit 62 sts along neckline.

Working in garter st, work [2 rows B, 2 rows A] twice, 2 rows B.

Bind off.

Button Band
With RS facing, smaller needles and B, pick up and knit 90 (92, 94, 96, 96, 98) sts along left front edge.

Complete same as for neckband.

Buttonhole Band
Mark positions for 7 evenly spaced buttonholes along right front edge, with the first and last being ½ inch from top and bottom.

With RS facing, smaller needles and B, pick up and knit 90 (92, 94, 96, 96, 98) sts along right front edge.

Working same garter-stripe pat as for button band, knit 5 rows.

Buttonhole row 1: With B, *knit to marked buttonhole position, bind off 4 sts; rep from * 6 times, knit to end.

Buttonhole row 2: With A, *knit to bound-off sts, cable cast on 5 sts; rep from * 6 times, knit to end.

Buttonhole row 3: With A, *knit to cast-on sts, k4, k2tog; rep from * 6 times, knit to end.

Knit 2 rows with B.

Bind off.

Set in sleeves.

Sew sleeve and side seams.

Sew on buttons opposite buttonholes. If desired, sew backing buttons to WS, going through both sets of buttonholes when sewing on main buttons. •

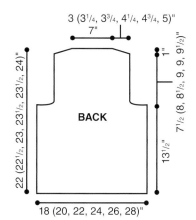

BACK

3 (3¼, 3¾, 4¼, 4¾, 5)"

7"

1"

7½ (8, 8½, 9, 9, 9½)"

22 (22½, 23, 23½, 23½, 24)"

13½"

18 (20, 22, 24, 26, 28)"

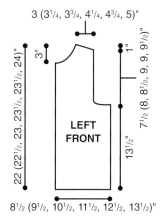

LEFT FRONT

3 (3¼, 3¾, 4¼, 4¾, 5)"

3"

1"

7½ (8, 8½, 9, 9, 9½)"

22 (22½, 23, 23½, 23½, 24)"

13½"

8½ (9½, 10½, 11½, 12½, 13½)"

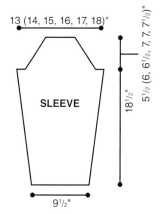

SLEEVE

13 (14, 15, 16, 17, 18)"

5½ (6, 6½, 7, 7, 7½)"

18½"

9½"

Part Three:
BEYOND THE BASICS

After mastering the essential closure techniques already discussed, you'll want to build on your skills. In this section, we'll explore a neat one-row buttonhole, super sturdy and flattering double-thick front bands and the ins and outs of double-breasted construction.

One-Row Buttonholes
Simple two-row buttonholes certainly do the trick, but here's a method that creates a buttonhole in a single row. It's quick to do and one of the neatest buttonholes imaginable.

Step 1: Work to the point where you want to begin your buttonhole. Slip the next stitch purlwise with the working yarn in the front.

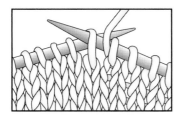

Step 2: Bring the working yarn to the back.

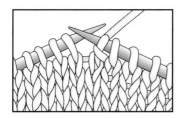

Step 3: Insert the right-hand needle into the first stitch on the left-hand needle and slip it purlwise onto the right-hand needle.

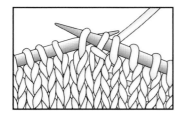

Step 4: Pass the second stitch on the right-hand needle over the first stitch to bind it off. That's one buttonhole stitch bound off.

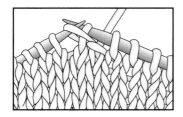

Step 5: Repeat Steps 3 and 4 as many times as is necessary to bind off the desired number of stitches for your buttonhole.

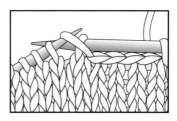

Step 6: After the last buttonhole stitch is bound off, slip the first stitch from the right-hand needle back to the left-hand needle.

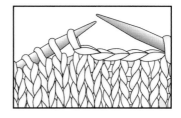

Step 7: Turn the work mid-row, so that the wrong side of the fabric is facing you.

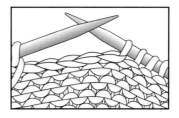

Step 8: Bring the yarn to the back, and use the cable cast-on method (see page 49) to cast on one more stitch than you bound off.

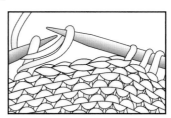

Step 9: Turn the work again, so that the right side of the fabric is facing you, and slip the first stitch on the left needle onto the right needle purlwise.

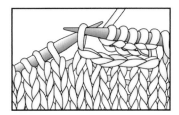

Step 10: Pass the second stitch on the right-hand needle over the first stitch on the right-hand needle to bind it off and complete the buttonhole.

CLOSURES UP CLOSE

Some knitters prefer the look of the one-row buttonhole when it is worked on wrong-side rows. Knitter's choice!

Double-Thick Front Bands
For an extra-sturdy border that will stabilize the front edges and prevent stretching, make double-thick front bands. They are worked at the same time as the knitting of the front pieces, as seen in the Funky Boyfriend Cardigan on page 37. Since these bands have two layers, two buttonholes are made on the same row—one for the button band and the other for the facing. Once the knitting is completed, the knit-in facing is folded to the wrong side along a slip-stitch crease line and is tacked down. Finally, the two buttonholes are joined using a simple buttonhole embroidery stitch, fusing them into one hole.

Step 1: Decide how wide you want your front band to be, then calculate how many stitches this will require. For example, for a 1-inch band worked at 5 stitches to the inch, the front band would be 5 stitches wide.

Step 2: Double the number in Step 1 (for the two band layers) and add one stitch (for the slipped stitch that will form the fold-over crease between the two band layers). In our example, this number would be (5 x 2) + 1 = 11 stitches.

Step 3: Knit the sweater front, placing a marker to separate the band stitches from the main knitting. Work them as follows:

On right-side rows: Knit across the band stitches, slipping the center crease stitch purlwise with the yarn in the back.

On wrong-side rows: Purl across all the band stitches, including the crease stitch.

Step 4: When it is time for a buttonhole, make one on both sides of the crease stitch. For instance, in the example above, you would work across the band stitches as follows: K1, bind off 3 stitches for the first buttonhole, k1, slip the next stitch purlwise for the crease, k1, bind off 3 stitches for the second buttonhole, k1. On the next row, cast on 3 stitches over both sets of bound-off stitches.

Double-Thick Button Band opened

Step 5: When the knitting is completed, fold the front band in half at the crease stitch and loosely whipstitch into place.

Double Thick Button Band closed

Step 6: Use embroidered buttonhole stitch to reinforce the buttonholes as follows:

Working from right to left, keep the yarn needle pointing toward the center of the buttonhole.

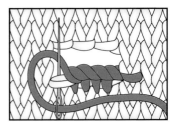

Double-Breasted Closures
This classic style for cardigans and jackets has two sets of buttonholes and overlapping fronts, and is used in the Double-Breasted Mosaic Cardi on page 42. This type of closure isn't difficult to knit, but it does require a bit of planning. Here's how:

Step 1: Determine how much the fronts will overlap. In our example, we'll have a 7-inch front overlap on a sweater with a back width of 20 inches.

Step 2: Subtract the width of the overlap from the width of the back, and then divide by two. In our example, this is $(20 - 7) \div 2 = 6\frac{1}{2}$.

Step 3: Add the width of the overlap to this number to determine the width of each front piece. In our example, $6\frac{1}{2} + 7 = 13\frac{1}{2}$ inches.

Step 4: Once the first front piece is completed (the left front in the case of a woman's garment), place markers for two sets of buttons.

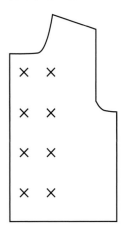

Step 5: When knitting the second front, use your preferred method to make buttonholes where marked. ●

This beautiful little jacket includes neat one-row buttonholes that are elegant and functional. The self-made buttons are the perfect finish!

Rebecca

Skill Level

● ● ● ▢ INTERMEDIATE

Sizes

Woman's small (medium, large, X-large, 2X-large, 3X-large)

Instructions are given for smallest size, with larger sizes in parentheses. When only 1 number is given, it applies to all sizes.

Finished Measurements

Chest (buttoned): 36 (40, 44, 48, 52, 56) inches
Length: 18 (18½, 19, 19½, 19½, 20) inches

Materials

- Plymouth Baby Alpaca Ampato (Aran weight; 100% baby alpaca; 128 yds/100g per skein): 7 (8, 8, 9, 9, 10) skeins tan #200
- Size 8 (5mm) knitting needles or size needed to obtain gauge
- Size 10 (6mm) knitting needles or size needed to obtain gauge
- 4 (⅞-inch) buttons

Gauge

16 sts and 28 rows = 4 inches/10cm in Box pat with smaller needles.

15 sts and 16 rows = 4 inches/10cm in Wave pat with larger needles.

To save time, take time to check gauge.

Pattern Stitches

Border (multiple of 11 sts)
Row 1 (RS): *[K2tog] twice, [yo, k1] 3 times, yo, [ssk] twice; rep from * to end.
Row 2: Knit.
Rep Rows 1 and 2 for pat.

Wave (multiple of 11 sts)
Row 1 (RS): *[K2tog] twice, [yo, k1] 3 times, yo, [ssk] twice; rep from * to end.
Row 2: Purl.
Row 3: Knit.
Row 4: Purl.
Rep Rows 1–4 for pat.

Garter Eyelet (odd number of sts)
Rows 1 (RS)–4: Purl.
Row 5: *K2tog, yo; rep from * to last st, k1.
Rows 6–10: Purl.

Box (multiple of 4 sts + 2)
Row 1 (RS): K2, *p2, k2; rep from * to end.
Row 2: P2, *k2, p2; rep from * to end.
Row 3: Rep Row 2.
Row 4: Rep Row 1.
Rep Rows 1–4 for pat.

Pattern Notes

Instructions include 1 selvage stitch at each side; these stitches are not reflected in the final measurements.

Work all shaping decreases 1 stitch from edge; when shaping in Box pattern, work either purl or knit decreases as necessary to maintain the pattern.

Back

With smaller needles, cast on 88 (99, 110, 121, 132, 143) sts.

Work 4 rows of Border pat.

Change to larger needles and Wave pat; work even until piece measures 5 (5½, 6, 6½, 6½, 7) inches, ending with Row 4 of Wave pat.

Change to smaller needles; work Row 1 of Garter Eyelet pat and dec 15 (18, 21, 24, 27, 30) sts evenly spaced across row—73 (81, 89, 97, 105, 113) sts rem.

Work Rows 2–10 of Garter Eyelet pat and on last row, inc 1 st—74 (82, 90, 98, 106, 114) sts.

Change to Box pat; work even until piece measures 10 inches or desired length to underarm, ending with a WS row.

Shape Armholes

Bind off 4 (5, 6, 7, 8, 9) sts at beg of next 2 rows, and 2 (2, 3, 3, 4, 4) sts at beg of following 2 rows—62 (68, 72, 78, 82, 88) sts.

Dec 1 st each side [every row] 1 (2, 1, 2, 1, 2) time(s), then [every other row] 4 (4, 5, 5, 6, 6) times—52 (56, 60, 64, 68, 72) sts.

Work even until armholes measure 6½ (7, 7½, 8, 8, 8½) inches, ending with a WS row.

Shape Neck

Row 1 (RS): Work 13 (15, 17, 19, 21, 23) sts; join 2nd ball of yarn and bind off 26 sts, work to end of row.

Working both sides at once with separate balls of yarn, dec 1 st each neck edge once—12 (14, 16, 18, 20, 22) sts each side.

Work even until armholes measure 7 (7½, 8, 8½, 8½, 9) inches, ending with a WS row.

Shape Shoulders

Bind off 4 (5, 5, 6, 7, 7) sts at beg of next 4 rows.

Bind off 4 (4, 6, 6, 6, 8) sts at beg of next 2 rows.

Left Front

With smaller needles, cast on 44 (44, 55, 55, 66, 66) sts.

Work 4 rows of Border pat.

Change to larger needles and Wave pat; work even until piece measures 5 (5½, 6, 6½, 6½, 7) inches, ending with Row 4 of Wave pat.

Change to smaller needles; work Row 1 of Garter Eyelet pat and dec 11 (7, 14, 10, 17, 13) sts evenly spaced across row—33 (37, 41, 45, 49, 53) sts.

Work Rows 2–10 of Garter Eyelet pat and on last row, inc 1 st—34 (38, 42, 46, 50, 54) sts.

Change to Box pat; work even until piece measures same as back to underarm, ending with a WS row.

Shape Armhole

At armhole edge, bind off 4 (5, 6, 7, 8, 9) sts once, and 2 (2, 3, 3, 4, 4) sts once—28 (31, 33, 36, 38, 41) sts.

Dec 1 st at armhole edge [every row] 1 (2, 1, 2, 1, 2) time(s), then [every other row] 4 (4, 5, 5, 6, 6) times—23 (25, 27, 29, 31, 33) sts.

Work even until armhole measures 5 (5½, 6, 6½, 6½, 7) inches, ending with a RS row.

Shape Neck
At neck edge, bind off 4 sts once, 3 sts once, and 2 sts once—14 (16, 18, 20, 22, 24) sts.

At neck edge, dec 1 st [every row] twice—12 (14, 16, 18, 20, 22) sts.

Work even until armhole measures same as back to shoulders, ending with a WS row.

Shape Shoulders
At armhole edge, bind off 4 (5, 5, 6, 7, 7) sts twice and 4 (4, 6, 8, 6, 8) sts once.

Right Front
Work as for left front to armhole, ending with a RS row.

Shape armhole as for left front, then work even until armhole measures same as left front to neck shaping, ending with a WS row.

Shape neck as for left front, then work even until armhole measures same as left front to shoulder shaping, ending with a RS row.

Shape shoulders as for left front.

Sleeves
With smaller needles, cast on 66 (66, 77, 77, 77, 77) sts.

Work 4 rows of Border pat.

Change to larger needles; work even in Wave Pat until piece measures 3 inches, ending with Row 4 of Wave pat.

Change to smaller needles; work Row 1 of Garter Eyelet pat and on first row, dec 3 (3, 6, 6, 6, 6) sts evenly spaced across row—63 (63, 71, 71, 71, 71) sts.

Work Rows 2–10 of Garter Eyelet pat and on last row, inc 3 (3, 7, 7, 7, 7) sts evenly spaced—66 (66, 78, 78, 78, 78) sts.

Change to Box pat; dec 1 st each side [every other row] 0 (0, 3, 0, 0, 0) times, [every 4 rows] 7 (1, 7, 7, 1, 0) time(s), [every 6 rows] 1 (5, 0, 1, 5, 0) time(s), [every 8 rows] 0 (0, 0, 0, 0, 3) times, and [every 10 rows] 0 (0, 0, 0, 0, 1) time(s)—50 (54, 58, 62, 66, 70) sts.

Work even until piece measures 10 inches or desired length to underarm, ending with a WS row.

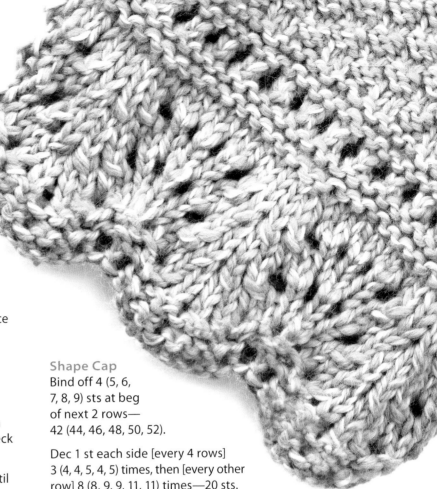

Shape Cap
Bind off 4 (5, 6, 7, 8, 9) sts at beg of next 2 rows—42 (44, 46, 48, 50, 52).

Dec 1 st each side [every 4 rows] 3 (4, 4, 5, 4, 5) times, then [every other row] 8 (8, 9, 9, 11, 11) times—20 sts.

Work 0 (0, 1, 1, 1, 0) row(s) even.

Bind off 2 sts at beg of next 4 rows—12 sts.

Bind off.

Finishing
Weave in ends.

Block pieces to measurements.

Sew shoulder seams.

Neckband
With RS facing and smaller needles, pick up and knit 74 sts along neckline.

Row 1 (WS): Knit.

Row 2: Purl.

Bind off kwise on WS.

Button Band
With RS facing and smaller needles, pick up and knit 66 (68, 70, 72, 72, 74) sts along left front edge.

Knit all rows until band measures 1 inch.

Bind off.

Buttonhole Band

Mark positions for 4 buttonholes along right front, with the first ½ inch from beg of front neck shaping, the last at the eyelet row and the others evenly spaced in between.

With RS facing and smaller needles, pick up and knit 66 (68, 70, 72, 72, 74) sts along right front edge.

Knit all rows until band measures ½ inch.

Buttonhole row: Knit, making 4-st 1-row buttonholes (see page 29) opposite markers.

Knit all rows until band measures 1 inch.

Bind off.

Set in sleeves.

Sew sleeve and side seams.

Make 4 knitted covered buttons (see page 54).

Sew on buttons opposite buttonholes. •

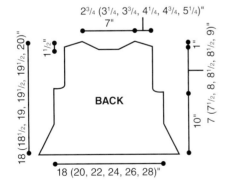

BACK

2³/₄ (3¹/₄, 3³/₄, 4¹/₄, 4³/₄, 5¹/₄)"

7"

1¹/₂"

1"

7 (7¹/₂, 8, 8¹/₂, 8¹/₂, 9)"

10"

18 (18¹/₂, 19, 19¹/₂, 19¹/₂, 20)"

18 (20, 22, 24, 26, 28)"

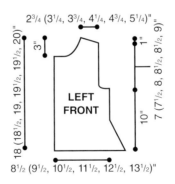

LEFT FRONT

2³/₄ (3¹/₄, 3³/₄, 4¹/₄, 4³/₄, 5¹/₄)"

3"

1"

7 (7¹/₂, 8, 8¹/₂, 8¹/₂, 9)"

10"

18 (18¹/₂, 19, 19¹/₂, 19¹/₂, 20)"

8¹/₂ (9¹/₂, 10¹/₂, 11¹/₂, 12¹/₂, 13¹/₂)"

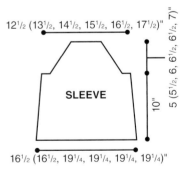

SLEEVE

12¹/₂ (13¹/₂, 14¹/₂, 15¹/₂, 16¹/₂, 17¹/₂)"

10"

5 (5¹/₂, 6, 6¹/₂, 6¹/₂, 7)"

16¹/₂ (16¹/₂, 19¹/₄, 19¹/₄, 19¹/₄, 19¹/₄)"

Double-thick bands add stability to a stress point in a garment, as seen in this updated Aran jacket. Here, smooth stockinette bands contrast with the cables and other textures.

Funky Boyfriend Cardigan

Skill Level
◼◼◼▢ INTERMEDIATE

Sizes
Woman's small (medium, large, X-large, 2X-large, 3X-large)

Instructions are given for smallest size, with larger sizes in parentheses. When only 1 number is given, it applies to all sizes.

Finished Measurements
Chest (buttoned): 38½ (42½, 44½, 48½, 50½, 54½) inches
Length: 24 (24, 24½, 24½, 25, 25) inches

Materials
- Rowan Felted Tweed Aran (Aran weight; 50% merino wool/25% alpaca/25% viscose; 95 yds/50g per ball): 14 (14, 15, 16, 17, 18) balls glade #733
- Size 8 (5mm) straight and 29-inch circular needles
- Size 9 (5.5mm) straight and 29-inch circular needles or size needed to obtain gauge
- Stitch markers
- Stitch holders
- Cable needle
- 7 (1-inch) buttons #12022 from JHB International

4 MEDIUM

Gauge
16 sts and 24 rows = 4 inches/10cm in Double Seed St with larger needles.

24 sts and 24 rows = 4 inches/10cm in Cable pat with larger needles.

To save time, take time to check gauge.

Special Abbreviations

Right Twist (RT): K2tog and leave on LH needle; insert RH needle between these 2 sts and knit the first st again.

2/2 Left Cross (2/2 LC): Sl 2 to cn and hold in front; k2, k2 from cn.

2/2 Right Cross (2/2 RC): Sl 2 to cn and hold in back; k2, k2 from cn.

Make 1 (M1): Inc by making a backward loop over RH needle.

Pattern Stitches

1x1 Rib (even number of sts)
Row 1: *K1, p1; rep from * to end.
Rep Row 1 for pat.

Double Seed St (even number of sts)
Rows 1 (RS) and 2: *K1, p1; rep from * to end.
Rows 3 and 4: *P1, k1; rep from * to end.
Rep Rows 1–4 for pat.

Cable (multiple of 12 sts + 6)
Note: A chart is provided for those preferring to work pat st from a chart.
Row 1 (RS): *P2, RT, p2, 2/2 RC, k2; rep from * to last 6 sts, p2, RT, p2.
Row 2: K2, p2, k2, *p6, k2, p2, k2; rep from * to end.
Row 3: *P2, RT, p2, k2, 2/2 LC; rep from * to last 6 sts, p2, RT, p2.
Row 4: Rep Row 2.
Rep Rows 1–4 for pat.

Pattern Note

All pieces are worked back and forth. Circular needles are used to accommodate stitches of larger pieces; do not join.

Back

With smaller circular needle, cast on 96 (104, 116, 124, 136, 144) sts.

Work in 1x1 Rib until piece measures 1½ inches, ending with a WS row, and on last row, inc 1 st each end—98 (106, 118, 126, 138, 146) sts.

Set-up row (RS): Change to larger circular needle; work 10 (14, 14, 18, 18, 22) sts in Double Seed St, pm, work 78 (78, 90, 90, 102, 102) sts in Cable pat, pm, work 10 (14, 14, 18, 18, 22) sts in Double Seed St.

Work even until piece measures 14½ inches or desired length to underarm, ending with a WS row.

Shape Armholes

Bind off 10 (12, 14, 16, 18, 20) sts at beg of next 2 rows—78 (82, 90, 94, 102, 106) sts.

Work even until armholes measure 6½ (6½, 7, 7, 7½, 7½) inches, ending with a WS row.

Shape Neck

Row 1 (RS): Work 12 (14, 18, 20, 24, 26) sts; join 2nd ball of yarn and bind off 54 sts; work to end of row.

Row 2: Working both sides at once with separate balls of yarn, work even.

Row 3: Work to 2 sts before neck edge, k2tog; ssk, work to end—11 (13, 17, 19, 23, 25) sts each side.

Work even until armholes measure 7 (7, 7½, 7½, 8, 8) inches, ending with a WS row.

Shape Shoulders

Bind off 4 (4, 6, 6, 8, 8) sts at beg of next 4 rows, then bind off 3 (5, 5, 7, 7, 9) sts at beg of last 2 rows.

Left Front

With smaller needles, cast on 61 (65, 65, 69, 69, 73).

Row 1 (RS): Work 50 (54, 54, 58, 58, 62) sts in 1x1 Rib, pm, k5, sl 1, k5.

Row 2: P11, work 1x1 Rib to end.

Rep Rows 1 and 2 until piece measures 1½ inches, ending with a WS row and on last row, inc 1 st at beg and end of rib section—63 (67, 67, 71, 71, 75) sts.

Set-up row (RS): Change to larger needles; work 10 (14, 14, 18, 18, 22) sts in Double Seed St, pm, work 42 sts in Cable pat, k5, sl 1, k5.

Row 2: P11, work Cable pat to marker, work Double Seed St to end of row.

Work even until piece measures same as back to underarm, ending with a WS row.

Shape Armhole

Bind off 10 (12, 14, 16, 18, 20) sts at beg of next row—53 (55, 53, 55, 53, 55) sts.

Work even until armhole measures ½ (½, 1, 1, 2, 2) inch(es), ending with a WS row.

Shape Neck

At neck edge, dec 1 st [every row] 24 (24, 12, 12, 0, 0) times, then [every RS row] 7 (7, 13, 13, 19, 19) times as follows:

Dec row (RS): Work in pat to last 14 sts, p2tog, p1, k5, sl 1, k5.

Dec row (WS): P11, k1, k2tog, work to end of row.

22 (24, 28, 30, 34, 36) sts rem after neck decs are complete.

Work even until armhole measures 7 (7, 7½, 7½, 8, 8) inches, ending with a WS row.

Shape Shoulder

At armhole edge, bind off 4 (4, 6, 6, 8, 8) sts twice, then 3 (5, 5, 7, 7, 9) sts once—11 sts.

Neckband

Work even until 11-st band measures approx 8 (8½, 9, 9½, 10, 10½) inches from shoulder.

Cut yarn, leaving a 20-inch tail. Slip sts to holder.

Mark positions for 7 evenly spaced buttons along left front, with the first ½ inch from lower edge, the last ½ inch from beg of front neck shaping and the others evenly spaced in between them.

Right Front

With smaller needles, cast on 61 (65, 65, 69, 69, 73).

Row 1 (RS): K5, sl 1, k5, pm, work 50 (54, 54, 58, 58, 62) sts in 1x1 Rib.

Row 2: Work 1x1 Rib to marker, p11.

Rep Rows 1 and 2 until piece measures ½ inch, ending with a WS row.

Buttonhole row 1 (RS): K1, bind off 3 sts, k1 (st on RH needle following last bound-off st), sl 1, k1, bind off 3 sts, k1 (st on RH needle following last bound-off st), work in rib to end of row.

Buttonhole row 2: [Work in pat to bound-off sts, cast on 3 sts] twice, k1.

Note: Rep Buttonhole rows opposite each marked button position on left front.

Work even until piece measures 1½ inches, ending with a WS row and on last row, inc 1 st at beg and end of rib section—63 (67, 67, 71, 71, 75) sts.

Set-up row (RS): Change to larger needles; k5, sl 1, k5, work 42 sts in Cable pat, pm, work 10 (14, 14, 18, 18, 22) sts in Double Seed St.

Row 2: Work Double Seed St to first marker, work Cable pat to next marker, p11.

Work even until piece measures same as back to underarm, ending with a RS row.

Shape Armhole

Bind off 10 (12, 14, 16, 18, 20) sts at beg of next row—53 (55, 53, 55, 53, 55) sts.

Work even until armhole measures ½ (½, 1, 1, 2, 2) inch(es), ending with a WS row.

Shape Neck

At neck edge, dec 1 st [every row] 24 (24, 12, 12, 0, 0) times, then [every RS row] 7 (7, 13, 13, 19, 19) times as follows:

Dec row (RS): K5, sl 1, k5, p1, p2tog, work in pat to end of row.

Dec row (WS): Work in pat to last 14 sts, k2tog, k1, p11.

22 (24, 28, 30, 34, 36) sts rem after neck dec are complete.

Work even until armhole measures 7 (7, 7½, 7½, 8, 8) inches, ending with a RS row.

Shape Shoulder

At armhole edge, bind off 4 (4, 6, 6, 8, 8) sts twice, then 3 (5, 5, 7, 7, 9) sts once—11 sts.

Neckband

Work even until 11-st band measures same as for left front.

Cut yarn, leaving a 20-inch tail. Slip sts to holder.

Sleeves

With smaller needles, cast on 56 sts.

Work in 1x1 Rib until piece measures 1½ inches, ending with a WS row, and on last row, inc 1 st each end—58 sts.

Set-up row (RS): Change to larger needles; work 2 sts in Double Seed St, pm, work 54 sts in Cable pat, pm, work 2 sts in Double Seed St.

Working new sts into established Double Seed St as they accumulate and maintaining Cable pat at center between markers, inc 1 st each side [every 4 rows] 0 (0, 0, 2, 9, 12) times, [every 6 rows] 2 (4, 15, 14, 9, 6) times, then [every 8 rows] 12 (10, 1, 0, 0, 0) time(s) as follows: k1, M1, work in pat to last st, M1, k1—86 (86, 90, 90, 94, 94) sts.

Work even until piece measures 22 (22, 21½, 21, 21, 20½) inches, ending with a WS row.

Saddle

Bind off 33 (33, 35, 35, 37, 37) sts at beg of next 2 rows—20 sts.

Work even until saddle measures 1¾ (2¼, 2¾, 3¼, 3¾, 4¼) inches, ending with a WS row.

Bind off in pat.

Finishing

Lightly block pieces.

Sew saddles between back and fronts, forming shoulders.

Test length of neckband to ensure that both sides meet at center back neck when slightly stretched; if too long, unravel a few rows; if too short, work a few more rows.

Graft left and right neckband sts using Kitchener st (see page 51).

Sew neck side of band to back neck.

Fold front bands in half at slip-st fold line and whipstitch to WS.

Set in sleeves.

Sew underarm and side seams.

Work buttonhole st (see page 31) to join the 2 sets of buttonholes.

Sew on buttons at marked positions opposite buttonholes. ●

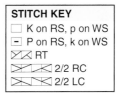

STITCH KEY
□ K on RS, p on WS
▬ P on RS, k on WS
▱ RT
▱ 2/2 RC
▱ 2/2 LC

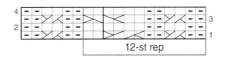

CABLE CHART

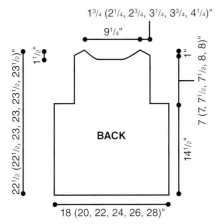

BACK

1¾ (2¼, 2¾, 3¼, 3¾, 4¼)"

9¼"

1½"

7 (7, 7½, 7½, 8, 8)"

1"

14½"

22½ (22½, 23, 23, 23½, 23½)"

18 (20, 22, 24, 26, 28)"

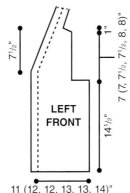

LEFT FRONT

7½"

1"

7 (7, 7½, 7½, 8, 8)"

14½"

11 (12, 12, 13, 13, 14)"

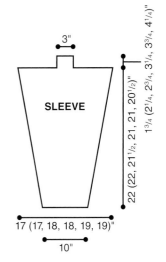

SLEEVE

3"

1¾ (2¼, 2¾, 3¼, 3¾, 4¼)"

22 (22, 21½, 21, 21, 20½)"

17 (17, 18, 18, 19, 19)"

10"

Don't let a double-breasted closure frighten you! This type of garment has twice as many buttonholes, but is not hard to make. Give this mosaic jacket a try and you'll see how easy they are to construct.

Double-Breasted Mosaic Cardi

Skill Level
■■■□ INTERMEDIATE

Sizes
Woman's small (medium, large, X-large, 2X-large, 3X-large)

Instructions are given for smallest size, with larger sizes in parentheses. When only 1 number is given, it applies to all sizes.

Finished Measurements
Chest (buttoned): 36 (39½, 41½, 45, 47½, 51) inches
Length: 18½ (19, 19½, 19½, 20, 20) inches

Materials
- Brown Sheep Company Lamb's Pride Bulky (chunky weight; 85% wool/15% mohair; 125 yds/4 oz per skein): 4 (5, 5, 5, 6, 6) skeins each deep pine #M172 (A) and seafoam #M16 (B)
- Size 11 (8mm) straight and 32-inch circular needles or size needed to obtain gauge.
- 8 buttons

Gauge
14 sts and 28 rows = 4 inches/10cm in Mosaic pat.

To save time, take time to check gauge.

Pattern Stitch
Mosaic (10-st rep)
See chart.

Special Technique
Double-Buttonhole Row (RS): Work 3 sts in established pat, bind off 3 sts, work 11 sts (including the st on the RH needle following the bind-off), bind off 3 sts, work to end of row. On following row, cast on 3 sts over the bound-off sts.

Pattern Notes
The Mosaic pattern is worked with a garter round and uses only 1 color per row; the pattern is formed by slipping stitches of the other color.

Always slip stitches with the yarn held to the wrong side.

Do not cut yarns when changing colors; carry yarn not in use neatly up the edge, twisting the colors at the beginning of each right-side row.

Some right-side rows end with slipped stitches. If working a "work-even" row, simply turn at the last stitch of the color in use and work back to the end of the wrong-side row. If shaping an edge, always work the last stitch with the working yarn. If working a decrease row, use the working yarn to work the decrease in the last 2 stitches, then knit the resulting stitch on the following row.

Work all decreases as k2tog at the beginning of rows and ssk at the end of rows.

When binding off, knit all stitches of the bind-off and on right-side rows, carry the other yarn along the bind-off so that it will be ready at the edge for the next right-side row.

Back
With A, cast on 63 (69, 73, 79, 83, 89) sts.

Change to B; beg and ending where indicated for your size on the chart, work even in Mosaic pat until piece measures 10 inches or desired length to underarm, ending after a WS row.

Note: Make a note of pat row on which you end.

Shape Armholes
Bind off 4 (5, 6, 6, 6, 7) sts at beg of next 2 rows, then bind off 2 (2, 2, 3, 3, 4) sts at beg of following 2 rows—51 (55, 57, 61, 65, 67) sts.

Dec 1 st at beg and end of next row, then [every row] 0 (1, 1, 3, 4, 4) more time(s), then [every other row] 3 (3, 3, 2, 2, 2) times—43 (45, 47, 49, 51, 53) sts.

Work even until armholes measure 7½ (8, 8½, 8½, 9, 9) inches, ending with a WS row.

Shape Shoulders
Bind off 2 (3, 3, 3, 4, 4) sts at beg of next 6 rows, then bind off 4 (2, 3, 4, 2, 3) sts at beg of following 2 rows—23 sts.

Bind off.

Left Front
With A, cast on 43 (46, 48, 51, 53, 56) sts.

Change to B; beg and ending where indicated for your size on chart, work even in Mosaic pat until piece measures same as back to underarm, ending with the same WS pat row as for back.

Shape Armholes
At armhole edge, bind off 4 (5, 6, 6, 6, 7) sts once and 2 (2, 2, 3, 3, 4) sts once—37 (39, 40, 42, 44, 45) sts.

At armhole edge, dec 1 st [every row] 1 (2, 2, 4, 5, 5) time(s), then [every other row] 3 (3, 3, 2, 2, 2) times—33 (34, 35, 36, 37, 38) sts.

Work even until armhole measures 5½ (6, 6½, 6½, 7, 7) inches, ending with a RS row.

Note: Make a note of pat row on which you end.

Shape Neck
At neck edge, bind off 11 sts once, 5 sts once and 3 sts once—14 (15, 16, 17, 18, 19) sts.

At neck edge, dec 1 st [every row] 4 times—10 (11, 12, 13, 14, 15) sts.

Work even until armhole measures same as for back, ending with a WS row.

Shape Shoulder
At armhole edge, bind off [2 (3, 3, 3, 4, 4) sts] 3 times, then [4 (2, 3, 4, 2, 3) sts] once.

Right Front
Note: Use left front to determine position of buttonhole rows for right front as follows: Mark positions for 3 buttonhole rows on the left front edge, with the first approx 8½ inches from the lower edge, the 3rd approx 7 inches above the first and the 2nd between the 2. Work Double-Buttonhole Rows at these positions when working right front.

Work same as for left front to underarm, ending 1 row before pat row noted at back armhole (this will be a RS row) and working Double-Buttonhole Row at marked positions throughout.

Shape armhole same as for left front to neck shaping, ending with a WS row.

Shape neck as for left front, ending with a RS row.

Shape shoulder as for left front.

Sleeves
Cast on 59 sts.

Change to B; beg and end Mosaic pat where indicated for sleeves on the chart.

Maintaining established pat, dec 1 st each side [every 10 rows] 6 (0, 0, 0, 0, 0) times, [every 12 rows] 0 (5, 0, 0, 0, 0) times, [every 14 rows] 0 (0, 4, 0, 0, 0) times, [every 16 rows] 0 (0, 0, 3, 0, 0) times, and [every 20 rows] 0 (0, 0, 0, 2, 1) time(s)—47 (49, 51, 53, 55, 57) sts.

Work even until piece measures 10 inches or desired length to underarm, ending with same WS pat row as for back at underarm.

Shape Cap
Bind off 4 (5, 6, 6, 6, 7) sts at beg of next 2 rows—39 (39, 39, 41, 43, 43) sts.

Dec 1 st each side [every 8 rows] 0 (1, 2, 0, 0, 0) time(s), [every 6 rows] 4 (4, 3, 5, 5, 5) times and [every 4 rows] 1 (0, 0, 1, 2, 2) time(s)—29 sts.

Work 0 (0, 1, 1, 1, 1) row(s) even.

Bind off 3 sts at beg of next 6 rows—11 sts.

Bind off.

Finishing
Weave in ends; lightly block pieces.

Sew shoulder seams.

Neckband

With RS facing, using circular needle and A, pick up and knit 83 sts along neckline, beg and ending at front edges.

Knit 1 row.

Beg with the pat row after the one you noted for front neck shaping, work Mosaic Pat for 2½ inches, ending with a WS row.

Next row (RS): Work Double-Buttonhole Row.

Next row: Cast on 3 sts over the bound-off sts of previous row.

Work even until neckband measures approx 3 inches, ending with a RS row.

Bind off kwise on WS.

Sew in sleeves.

Sew underarm and side seams.

Sew buttons on left front aligning with buttonholes on right front. ●

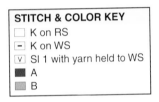

STITCH & COLOR KEY

- ☐ K on RS
- ⊟ K on WS
- Ⓥ Sl 1 with yarn held to WS
- ■ A
- ▨ B

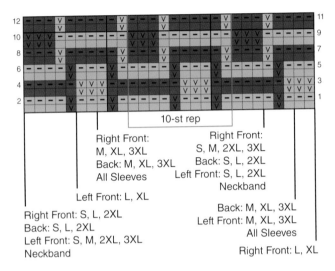

12
10
8
6
4
2
11
9
7
5
3
1
10-st rep
Right Front: M, XL, 3XL
Back: M, XL, 3XL
All Sleeves
Right Front: S, M, 2XL, 3XL
Back: S, L, 2XL
Left Front: S, L, 2XL
Neckband
Left Front: L, XL
Back: M, XL, 3XL
Left Front: M, XL, 3XL
All Sleeves
Right Front: S, L, 2XL
Back: S, L, 2XL
Left Front: S, M, 2XL, 3XL
Neckband
Right Front: L, XL

MOSAIC CHART

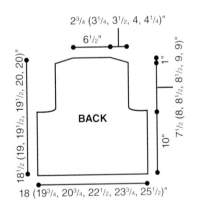

2¾ (3¼, 3½, 4, 4¼)"
6½"
BACK
18½ (19, 19½, 19½, 20, 20)"
1"
7½ (8, 8½, 8½, 9, 9)"
10"
18 (19¾, 20¾, 22½, 23¾, 25½)"

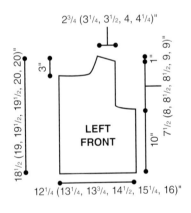

2¾ (3¼, 3½, 4, 4¼)"
3"
LEFT FRONT
18½ (19, 19½, 19½, 20, 20)"
1"
7½ (8, 8½, 8½, 9, 9)"
10"
12¼ (13¼, 13¾, 14½, 15¼, 16)"

3¼"
SLEEVE
15 (15½, 16, 16, 16½, 16½)"
10"
5 (5½, 6, 6, 6½, 6½)"
13½ (14, 14½, 15¼, 15¾, 16¼)"
16¾"

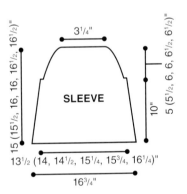

General Information

Abbreviations & Symbols

[ ] work instructions within brackets as many times as directed

( ) work instructions within parentheses in the place directed

** repeat instructions following the asterisks as directed

* repeat instructions following the single asterisk as directed

" inch(es)

approx approximately
beg begin/begins/beginning
CC contrasting color
ch chain stitch
cm centimeter(s)
cn cable needle
dec(s) decrease/decreases/decreasing
dpn(s) double-point needle(s)
g gram(s)
inc(s) increase/increases/increasing

k knit
k2tog knit 2 stitches together
kfb knit in front and back
kwise knitwise
LH left hand
m meter(s)
M1 make one stitch
MC main color
mm millimeter(s)
oz ounce(s)
p purl
p2tog purl 2 stitches together
pat(s) pattern(s)
pm place marker
psso pass slipped stitch over
pwise purlwise
rem remain/remains/remaining
rep(s) repeat(s)
rev St st reverse stockinette stitch
RH right hand
rnd(s) rounds
RS right side

skp slip, knit, pass slipped stitch over—1 stitch decreased
sk2p slip 1, knit 2 together, pass slipped stitch over the knit 2 together—2 stitches decreased
sl slip
sl 1 kwise slip 1 knitwise
sl 1 pwise slip 1 purlwise
sl st slip stitch(es)
ssk slip, slip, knit these 2 stitches together—a decrease
st(s) stitch(es)
St st stockinette stitch
tbl through back loop(s)
tog together
WS wrong side
wyib with yarn in back
wyif with yarn in front
yd(s) yard(s)
yfwd yarn forward
yo (yo's) yarn over(s)

Skill Levels

BEGINNER

Beginner projects for first-time knitters using basic stitches. Minimal shaping.

EASY

Easy projects using basic stitches, repetitive stitch patterns, simple color changes and simple shaping and finishing.

INTERMEDIATE

Intermediate projects with a variety of stitches, mid-level shaping and finishing.

EXPERIENCED

Experienced projects using advanced techniques and stitches, detailed shaping and refined finishing.

Standard Yarn Weight System
Categories of yarn, gauge ranges, and recommended needle sizes

Yarn Weight Symbol & Category Names	1 SUPER FINE	2 FINE	3 LIGHT	4 MEDIUM	5 BULKY	6 SUPER BULKY
Type of Yarns in Category	Sock, Fingering, Baby	Sport, Baby	DK, Light Worsted	Worsted, Afghan, Aran	Chunky, Craft, Rug	Bulky, Roving
Knit Gauge Range* in Stockinette Stitch to 4 inches	27–32 sts	23–26 sts	21–24 sts	16–20 sts	12–15 sts	6–11 sts
Recommended Needle in Metric Size Range	2.25–3.25mm	3.25–3.75mm	3.75–4.5mm	4.5–5.5mm	5.5–8mm	8mm and larger
Recommended Needle U.S. Size Range	1 to 3	3 to 5	5 to 7	7 to 9	9 to 11	11 and larger

* GUIDELINES ONLY: The above reflect the most commonly used gauges and needle sizes for specific yarn categories.

Inches Into Millimeters & Centimeters
All measurements are rounded off slightly.

inches	mm	cm	inches	cm	inches	cm	inches	cm
1/8	3	0.3	5	12.5	21	53.5	38	96.5
1/4	6	0.6	5½	14	22	56.0	39	99.0
3/8	10	1.0	6	15.0	23	58.5	40	101.5
1/2	13	1.3	7	18.0	24	61.0	41	104.0
5/8	15	1.5	8	20.5	25	63.5	42	106.5
3/4	20	2.0	9	23.0	26	66.0	43	109.0
7/8	22	2.2	10	25.5	27	68.5	44	112.0
1	25	2.5	11	28.0	28	71.0	45	114.5
1¼	32	3.2	12	30.5	29	73.5	46	117.0
1½	38	3.8	13	33.0	30	76.0	47	119.5
1¾	45	4.5	14	35.5	31	79.0	48	122.0
2	50	5.0	15	38.0	32	81.5	49	124.5
2½	65	6.5	16	40.5	33	84.0	50	127.0
3	75	7.5	17	43.0	34	86.5		
3½	90	9.0	18	46.0	35	89.0		
4	100	10.0	19	48.5	36	91.5		
4½	115	11.5	20	51.0	37	94.0		

Cast-On

Leaving an end about an inch long for each stitch to be cast on, make a slip knot on the right needle.

Place the thumb and index finger of your left hand between the yarn ends with the long yarn end over your thumb, and the strand from the skein over your index finger. Close your other fingers over the strands to hold them against your palm. Spread your thumb and index fingers apart and draw the yarn into a "V."

Place the needle in front of the strand around your thumb and bring it underneath this strand. Carry the needle over and under the strand on your index finger.

Draw through loop on thumb.

Drop the loop from your thumb and draw up the strand to form a stitch on the needle.

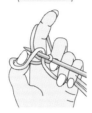

Repeat until you have cast on the number of stitches indicated in the pattern. Remember to count the beginning slip knot as a stitch.

Cable Cast-On

This type of cast-on is used when adding stitches in the middle or at the end of a row.

Make a slip knot on the left needle. Knit a stitch in this knot and place it on the left needle. Insert the right needle between the last two stitches on the left needle. Knit a stitch and place it on the left needle. Repeat for each stitch needed.

Knit (k)

Insert tip of right needle from front to back in next stitch on left needle.

Bring yarn under and over the tip of the right needle.

Pull yarn loop through the stitch with right needle point.

Slide the stitch off the left needle. The new stitch is on the right needle.

Purl (p)

With yarn in front, insert tip of right needle from back to front through next stitch on the left needle.

Bring yarn around the right needle counterclockwise. With right needle, draw yarn back through the stitch.

Slide the stitch off the left needle. The new stitch is on the right needle.

Bind-Off

Binding off (knit)

Knit first two stitches on left needle. Insert tip of left needle into first stitch worked on right needle and pull it over the second stitch and completely off the needle.

Knit the next stitch and repeat. When one stitch remains on right needle, cut yarn and draw tail through last stitch to fasten off.

Binding off (purl)

Purl first two stitches on left needle. Insert tip of left needle into first stitch worked on right needle and pull it over the second stitch and completely off the needle.

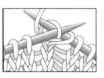

Purl the next stitch and repeat. When one stitch remains on right needle, cut yarn and draw tail through last stitch to fasten off.

Increase (inc)

Two stitches in one stitch

Increase (knit)

Knit the next stitch in the usual manner, but don't remove the stitch from the left needle. Place right needle behind left needle and knit again into the back of the same stitch. Slip original stitch off left needle.

Increase (purl)

Purl the next stitch in the usual manner, but don't remove the stitch from the left needle. Place right needle behind left needle and purl again into the back of the same stitch. Slip original stitch off left needle.

Invisible Increase (M1)

There are several ways to make or increase one stitch.

Make 1 with Left Twist (M1L)

Insert left needle from front to back under the horizontal loop between the last stitch worked and next stitch on left needle.

With right needle, knit into the back of this loop.

To make this increase on the purl side, insert left needle in same manner and purl into the back of the loop.

Make 1 with Right Twist (M1R)

Insert left needle from back to front under the horizontal loop between the last stitch worked and next stitch on left needle.

With right needle, knit into the front of this loop.

To make this increase on the purl side, insert left needle in same manner and purl into the front of the loop.

Make 1 with Backward Loop over the right needle

With your thumb, make a loop over the right needle.

Slip the loop from your thumb onto the needle and pull to tighten.

Make 1 in top of stitch below

Insert tip of right needle into the stitch on left needle one row below.

Knit this stitch, then knit the stitch on the left needle.

Decrease (dec)

Knit 2 together (k2tog)

Put tip of right needle through next two stitches on left needle as to knit. Knit these two stitches as one.

Purl 2 together (p2tog)

Put tip of right needle through next two stitches on left needle as to purl. Purl these two stitches as one.

Slip, Slip, Knit (ssk)

Slip next two stitches, one at a time as to knit, from left needle to right needle.

Insert left needle in front of both stitches and knit them together.

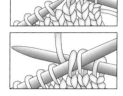

Slip, Slip, Purl (ssp)

Slip next two stitches, one at a time as to knit, from left needle to right needle. Slip these stitches back onto left needle keeping them twisted. Purl these two stitches together through back loops.

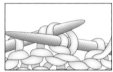

Kitchener Stitch

This method of weaving with two needles is used for the toes of socks and flat seams. To weave the edges together and form an unbroken line of stockinette stitch, divide all stitches evenly onto two knitting needles— one behind the other. Thread yarn into tapestry needle. Hold needles with wrong sides together and work from right to left as follows:

Step 1: Insert tapestry needle into first stitch on front needle as to purl. Draw yarn through stitch, leaving stitch on knitting needle.

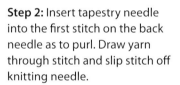
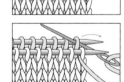

Step 2: Insert tapestry needle into the first stitch on the back needle as to purl. Draw yarn through stitch and slip stitch off knitting needle.

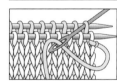

Step 3: Insert tapestry needle into the next stitch on same (back) needle as to knit, leaving stitch on knitting needle.

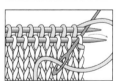

Step 4: Insert tapestry needle into the first stitch on the front needle as to knit. Draw yarn through stitch and slip stitch off knitting needle.

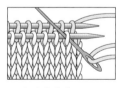

Step 5: Insert tapestry needle into the next stitch on same (front) needle as to purl. Draw yarn through stitch, leaving stitch on knitting needle.

Repeat Steps 2 through 5 until one stitch is left on each needle. Then repeat Steps 2 and 4. Fasten off. Woven stitches should be the same size as adjacent knitted stitches.

Pick Up & Knit

Step 1: With right side facing, working 1 st in from edge, insert tip of needle in space between first and second stitch.

Step 2: Wrap yarn around needle. (We show a contrasting color, but you will want to use the same yarn you used for your project.)

Step 3: Pull loop through to front.

Step 4: Repeat Steps 1–3.

Step 1

Step 2

Step 3

Step 4

3-Needle Bind-Off

Use this technique for seaming two edges together, such as when joining a seam. Hold the live edge stitches on two separate needles with right sides of the fabric together.

With a third needle, knit together a stitch from the front needle with one from the back.

Repeat, knitting a stitch from the front needle with one from the back needle once more.

Slip the first stitch over the second.

Repeat, knitting a front and back pair of stitches together, then bind one pair off.

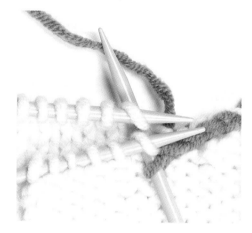

Crochet Stitches

Chain (ch)

Yarn over, pull through loop on hook.

Chain Stitch

Reverse Single Crochet (reverse sc)

Chain 1. Skip first stitch. Working from left to right, insert hook in next stitch from front to back, draw up loop on hook, yarn over, and draw through both loops on hook.

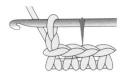

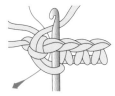

Reverse Single Crochet

Single Crochet (sc)

Insert the hook in the second chain through the center of the V. Bring the yarn over the hook from back to front.

Draw the yarn through the chain stitch and onto the hook.

Again bring yarn over the hook from back to front and draw it through both loops on hook.

For additional rows of single crochet, insert the hook under both loops of the previous stitch instead of through the center of the V as when working into the chain stitch.

Single Crochet

Choosing Buttons

Depending on the effect you desire, buttons can become a prominent part of a garment's design or can remain utilitarian and simply fade into the fabric. Whether they blend into the background or stand out, be sure to select appropriate buttons.

- Choose very large buttons when working with bulky yarns and smaller ones when working with finer yarns.

- If the knitted fabric is delicate, be sure the buttons aren't too heavy or else their weight will hang and stretch the fabric.

- Be sure the buttons aren't too small for the buttonholes. It's better to have a snug fit than a loose one!

- Try to match the laundering instructions for the buttons with those for the knitted garment. Otherwise, you'll have to remove the buttons each time the piece is cleaned.

DESIGNER'S TIP

CLOSURES UP CLOSE

To make button selection easy, knit a little swatch of fabric in the garment yarn, including a sample buttonhole. Take the swatch shopping with you and test out the buttons you like on the fabric.

Make Your Own Buttons
Sometimes it is difficult to find the perfect button to match a knitted project. There's an obvious (and easy) solution: Make your own! Here's how.

Knitted Button
Step 1: Cast on 1 stitch.

Step 2: Begin stockinette stitch (or even garter stitch), and increase one stitch each side every row by working into the front and back of each edge stitch until the piece measures approximately twice the desired diameter of the button.

Step 3: Work even until the piece measures the desired width of the button.

Step 4: Decrease one stitch each side every row until one stitch remains.

Step 5: Fasten off, leaving a 6- to 8-inch tail.

Stuff a little bit of matching yarn inside the button to fill it out. Use the yarn tail to sew on the button.

Crocheted Button
Step 1: Using an appropriate-size crochet hook, chain 2.

Step 2: Work 6 single crochet stitches (sc) into the second chain from the hook.

Step 3: Work 2 sc into each sc of the previous round—12 sc total.

Step 4: Repeat Step 3 until the button is the desired width.

Step 5: Work single crochet decrease stitches (sc dec) to combine every 2 stitches until 6 stitches remain.

Step 6: Fasten off, leaving a 6- to 8-inch tail.

Stuff a little bit of matching yarn inside the button to fill it out. Use the yarn tail to sew on the button.

How to Sew Buttons on Securely
To sew on a button, follow these steps:

Step 1: Choose matching thread and a pointy sewing needle that will fit through the holes in the button. Double the thread and tie a knot approximately 1 inch from the end. Attach the yarn where the button is to be located.

DESIGNER'S TIP

CLOSURES UP CLOSE

It's a good idea to purchase an extra button to sew onto the side seam on the wrong side of the garment. This way, if one button is lost, another one is at the ready!

Step 2: Hold the button in the desired location, and draw the threaded sewing needle through one of the holes on the button.

Step 3: Go through all the holes in the button several times to secure it, then create a shank by bringing the needle up from the wrong side of the fabric to the space between the button and the fabric, then wrapping the yarn around the sewing that attached the button.

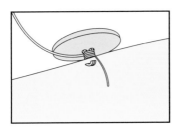

Step 4: Bring the needle back down to the wrong side of the front and tie a knot to secure it.

Meet the Designer

Melissa Leapman has published patterns in every premier needlecraft publication in the country. As a freelance designer, she's worked with leading ready-to-wear manufacturers and design houses in New York City. In addition, most American yarn companies commission Melissa to create designs promoting their new and existing yarns each season.

Melissa is the author of several best-selling knitting and crocheting books. Recent titles are *Cables Untangled, Continuous Cables, Color Knitting the Easy Way, Mastering Color Knitting* and *Stashbuster Knits.*

Leapman has been a featured guest on numerous television shows, is a popular guest blogger and is the host of several Leisure Arts knitting and crocheting DVDs. Her workshops are popular with crafters of all skill levels.

Resources

Many of the yarns and buttons can be found in your local yarn shop. If there isn't one in your area, contact the wholesaler below for more information.

Bejeweled & Bedazzled
105 Guildwood Parkway #11015
Toronto, ON
M1E 1P1 Canada
www.bejeweled-bedazzled.ca

Berroco Inc.
1 Tupperware Drive, Suite 4
N. Smithfield, RI 02896-6815
(401) 769-1212
www.berroco.com

Brown Sheep Co.
100662 County Road 16
Mitchell, NE 69357-2136
(800) 826-9136
www.brownsheep.com

Cascade Yarns
1224 Andover Park E.
Tukwila, WA 98188-3905
(206) 574-0440
www.cascadeyarns.com

Classic Elite Yarns
16 Esquire Road, Unit 2
North Billerica, MA 08162-2500
(800) 343-0308
www.classiceliteyarns.com

Dill Buttons of America
50 Choate Circle
Montoursville, PA 17754
(888) 460-7555
us.dill-buttons.com

JHB International Inc.
1955 S. Quince St.
Denver, CO 80231-3206
(800) 525-9007
www.buttons.com

Lion Brand Yarn
135 Kero Road
Carlstadt, NJ 07072
(800) 258-9276
www.lionbrand.com

Plymouth Yarn Co. Inc.
500 Lafayette St.
Bristol, PA 19007-0028
(215) 788-0459
www.plymouthyarn.com

Rowan
Distributed by Royal Yarns
International
404 Barnside Place
Rockville, MD 20850
(886) 621-7779
www.royalyarns.com

HOUSE of
WHITE
BIRCHES
PUBLISHERS
SINCE 1947

Cadigans & Closures is published by Annie's, 306 East Parr Road, Berne, IN 46711. Printed in USA. Copyright © 2012 Annie's. All rights reserved. This publication may not be reproduced in part or in whole without written permission from the publisher.

RETAIL STORES: If you would like to carry this pattern book or any other Annie's publications, visit AnniesWSL.com.

Every effort has been made to ensure that the instructions in this pattern book are complete and accurate. We cannot, however, take responsibility for human error, typographical mistakes or variations in individual work. Please visit AnniesCustomerCare.com to check for pattern updates.

ISBN: 978-1-59217-365-5

1 2 3 4 5 6 7 8 9

Photo Index

6

11

19

24

32

37

42